Description

At its core, Computer Science is the exploration of the principles and techniques that enable us to harness the power of computers. It encompasses a diverse set of skills and knowledge, ranging from the art of coding, where instructions are given to machines, to the intricate design of algorithms that solve complex problems. Computer Science is about understanding the architecture of computers, how data is stored and processed, and how networks facilitate communication between machines.

Most important

Why should I care?

Computer science is not just about programming; it's about acquiring a set of skills and knowledge that are increasingly fundamental to success in the modern world. It empowers individuals to think critically, solve problems, and participate actively in the digital age.

Understanding the basics of computer science is akin to being literate in the digital language. It empowers individuals to navigate technology confidently, be it using software, understanding algorithms, or making informed decisions about online security and privacy.

What do computer scientists do?

Computer scientists are the experts who design and build the digital tools we use every day. They write instructions, called code, that tell computers how to do all sorts of tasks. From creating software for your phone to making websites and improving security, computer scientists make technology work for us. They're the problem-solvers behind the scenes, making our digital world more efficient, faster, and better.

What types of problems do they work on?

Computer scientists work on a variety of problems in the digital world. They tackle challenges like creating new software and applications, designing websites, making sure our data is secure, and finding ways to use computers to solve real-life issues. Whether it's improving how technology works or inventing new ways for us to interact with computers, their focus is on making our digital experiences better and addressing the needs of the ever-evolving tech landscape.

What approaches do they use to solve those problems?

Computer scientists use a range of approaches to solve problems in the digital realm. Here are some common strategies:

1. **Algorithmic Thinking:** They devise step-by-step procedures (algorithms) to solve specific tasks efficiently. It's like creating a recipe for the computer to follow.
2. **Coding and Programming:** They write code in various programming languages to instruct computers. Coding is the language computers understand, and it's how they bring ideas to life.
3. **Data Analysis:** They examine and interpret data to gain insights. This helps them make informed decisions, improve systems, and understand patterns.

4. **Prototyping and Testing:** They often build prototypes of software or applications to test and refine ideas. This iterative process allows them to improve and perfect their solutions.
5. **Problem Decomposition:** They break down complex problems into smaller, more manageable parts. This makes it easier to understand and solve each component.
6. **Collaboration:** Computer scientists frequently work in teams. They share ideas, divide tasks, and bring different expertise to the table to solve problems efficiently.
7. **Continuous Learning:** Technology evolves rapidly, so computer scientists have to stay curious and continually learn. They adapt to new tools, languages, and methodologies to stay at the forefront of their field.

These approaches help them devise creative solutions to a wide range of challenges in the digital domain.

How to become a computer scientist?

There are two ways:

1. **The Traditional Approach:**

    a. Obtain a degree in Computer Science.
    b. Find a job related to your degree.
    c. You're done!

2. **The New Approach:**

a. Identify the specific area of Computer Science that interests you the most, such as robotics, networking, coding, and more.
b. Experiment with different aspects to discover what resonates with you.
c. Choose between getting a degree in your chosen category or pursuing a general Computer Science degree. Alternatively, explore self-learning paths through numerous online courses, many of which are free.
d. Keep in mind that while some tech companies prefer a degree, many others value experience just as much. As you gain experience, your qualifications become more significant than whether you have a degree.
e. Apply to jobs that align with your interests. Utilize platforms like LinkedIn, which has proven helpful for many entering the tech industry.

Both paths offer viable routes into the world of computer science, allowing individuals to tailor their journey based on their preferences and goals.

Quick history

- **1940s-1950s:** The Start of Computers Picture the birth of the first electronic computers, like ENIAC in the 1940s, marking the beginning of modern computers. A guy named John von Neumann introduced the concept of stored-program computers, like the brain behind how computers operate.

- **1950s-1960s:** Simplifying Computer Communication In the 1950s and 60s, people made it simpler to communicate with computers by creating languages like FORTRAN and LISP—like giving computers their own unique language. Around this time, they started connecting computers, a bit like the early version of the internet known as ARPANET.

- **1960s-1970s:** Computers Get Compact Fast forward to the 60s and 70s, and computers started getting smaller, small enough to sit on your desk! Companies like Microsoft emerged, introducing MS-DOS to make computers user-friendly.

- **1980s-1990s:** User-Friendly Computers In the 80s and 90s, computers became even more user-friendly with the introduction of pictures and icons—transforming a complex machine into something understandable with visuals. Tim Berners-Lee created the World Wide Web in the late 80s, making information-sharing more accessible.

- **1990s-2000s:** Computers Everywhere Imagine computers no longer confined to homes but everywhere, even fitting in your pocket! Smartphones and devices like the Palm Pilot made this possible. The internet became a vast library, offering access to almost anything.

- **2000s-Present:** Cloud Computing and Super Smart Computers Jump to the 2000s, and your computer can be in the sky! Cloud computing enables computer use without having one physically in front of you. Computers are becoming exceptionally smart, capable of learning and interacting with you—think of them as super smart companions assisting you.

How do things work?

How computers work?

1. Brainy

Computers are like really smart problem solvers. Think of the Central Processing Unit (CPU) as the brain doing all the hard thinking.

2. Binary

Computers talk in a special code made up of just two numbers: 1 and 0. It's like a yes (1) or no (0) language that helps computers say what they need to say.

3. Memory

Memory is like the computer's short-term memory where it keeps things handy. When you use a program or open a file, it goes into this memory for quick access.

4. Programs

Programs are sets of instructions for the computer, like following a recipe. These instructions are written in a language called code. When you use an app or play a game, your computer is following these instructions to make things happen.

5. Input and Output

Computers take in input, like when you type on a keyboard or touch the screen. They process this input and then show you the result on the screen—that's the output.

6. Storage Space

Your computer has a long-term memory called storage. It's like a big closet where it keeps all your files, photos, and games, even when you turn it off. Hard drives or solid-state drives are like the shelves in this closet.

7. Networks

Computers can talk to each other, like friends chatting. This happens through networks—either the internet or local networks. When you send a message or open a website, your computer is talking to another one somewhere in the world.

8. Graphics and Sound:

Computers can create visuals and sounds. There's a part called the Graphics Processing Unit (GPU) that's like an artist. It draws the pictures you see on the screen and makes games look cool.

9. Updates and Upgrades:

Computers need updates to learn new things or fix problems. Sometimes, you need new parts (like a better graphics card) to keep up with the latest stuff

10. The Internet:

When you're online, it's like your computer is using a magical highway—the internet. It connects with other computers, pulls in information, and sends your requests all around the globe.

This is just a basic overview to help you understand how computers work beyond the surface, showing the cool stuff that makes our digital world.

Understanding How Computers Work: A House Analogy

House	Computer
The Architect	**Computer and Software Engineers**
Similar to an architect planning a house, computer and software engineers design how computer components will work together.	Engineers map out the structure, ensuring seamless interaction among computer parts.
The Building	**Hardware (CPU, GPU, etc.)**
The building represents the physical components of a computer – walls, floors, structures. CPU, GPU, motherboard, and other parts form the architectural foundation.	Computer parts are the hardware that makes up the functional structure of a computer.
Interior Design	**Operating System**

Think of the operating system as the interior designer. Having a building is great, but the OS arranges everything inside, making sure it's functional and organized.	The operating system manages resources, ensuring applications run smoothly and coordinating interactions between hardware and software.
Furniture	**Applications and Programs**
Applications are like furniture, each serving a specific purpose. Just as a sofa is designed for comfort, programs have distinct goals.	Programs and applications provide functionality and user experiences, much like furniture adds purpose and comfort to a house.
Plumbing and Wiring	**Data Communication**
Plumbing and wiring are like data communication within a computer. Pipes and wires ensure water and electricity flow where needed.	Data communication facilitates the flow of information between different components of a computer.
Security System	**Cybersecurity Measures**
A security system protects your home; similarly, cybersecurity measures	Cybersecurity measures defend against unauthorized access, ensuring the integrity

safeguard a computer from potential threats.	and safety of computer systems.
Renovations and Updates	**Software Upgrades**
Renovations and updates represent software upgrades. Just as you enhance a house over time, software updates improve functionality.	Regular software updates introduce new features, fix bugs, and enhance overall performance.

How does the Internet work?

1. Digital Neighborhood:

- Imagine the internet as a massive digital neighborhood where computers, like houses, connect and communicate. Each computer has a unique address called an IP address, just like houses have street addresses.

2. Information Packets:

- When you send or request information on the internet, it's like mailing a letter. But instead of one big envelope, the information is divided into smaller packets. Each packet carries a piece of the message.

3. Routers - the Post Offices:

- Routers are like post offices in the digital neighborhood. They direct the information packets from your computer to the right destination. They check the address on each packet and send it on its way.

4. The World Wide Web - Your Digital Mall:

- The World Wide Web (www) is like a massive digital mall within the internet neighborhood. Websites are like different stores, and each web page is a product in that store. When you type a web address, your computer asks routers to find that specific store.

5. Web Servers - Storekeepers:

- Web servers are like the storekeepers. They hold all the information (web pages, images, videos) and wait for your computer to request something. When you click a link or enter a website, your computer asks the web server for the information.

6. Protocols - the Internet Rules:

- Protocols are like the rules everyone follows in the internet neighborhood. HTTP (Hypertext Transfer Protocol) is the rule for transferring web pages, while HTTPS adds security with encryption.

7. DNS - The Internet's Phone Book:

- DNS (Domain Name System) is like the phone book of the internet. When you type a web address, DNS translates it into the IP address of the server, helping your computer find the right digital store.

8. Modems and ISPs - Your Internet Connection:

- Your computer connects to the internet through a modem, and your Internet Service Provider (ISP) is like the utility company providing your connection. The faster the connection, the quicker you can access and send information.

9. Wireless Networks - Digital Roads:

- Wireless networks are like roads in the digital neighborhood. They allow your devices to connect without physical cables. Wi-Fi is like a digital sidewalk, enabling your devices to roam freely.

10. Cybersecurity - Digital Security Guards:

- Cybersecurity is like having security guards in the digital neighborhood. Firewalls, antivirus programs, and encryption help protect your information and keep unwanted visitors out.

How does the browser work?

1. The Library Card (URL):

- When you type a website address (URL) into the browser, it's like using a library card. The browser reads the card and knows exactly which "book" (webpage) you want to read.

2. The Librarian (DNS):

- The browser has a friendly librarian called DNS (Domain Name System). This librarian translates the website address you typed (like www.example.com) into the computer-friendly IP address, helping your browser find the right "shelf" (web server) in the library.

3. The Journey Begins (Request and Response):

- Your browser sends a request to the web server, asking for the web page. It's like sending a note to the librarian asking for a specific book. The web server, being the helpful librarian, sends back the requested webpage (book) as a response.

4. Assembling the Page (HTML, CSS, and JavaScript):

- The webpage isn't just one big file; it's like a puzzle made up of HTML (structure), CSS (style), and JavaScript (interactivity). The browser puts all these pieces together, creating the beautiful webpage you see. It's like assembling a book with text, pictures, and interactive elements.

5. Rendering (Displaying) the Page:

- The browser is your reading companion. It reads the assembled webpage and displays it on your screen. It's like your magic glasses showing you the content in a way that's easy to read and interact with.

6. Cookies - Leaving Sticky Notes:

- Cookies are like little sticky notes your browser leaves behind. They contain information about your visit, helping websites remember your preferences or login status. It's like leaving a note in the library about the books you've read.

7. Security Guards (SSL/TLS):

- If you're on a secure site (https://), it means the information exchanged between your browser and the web server is encrypted. It's like having security guards ensuring your conversations in the library remain private and secure.

How does the AI work?

1. **Learning from Examples - Machine Learning:**
   - **Everyday Comparison:** Think of AI as a learner. Machine learning, a part of AI, is like teaching it using examples. Show it pictures of cats, and it learns to recognize other cats.
2. **Making Predictions - Predictive Modeling:**
   - **Everyday Comparison:** AI makes predictions based on what it learns. Imagine predicting the

weather by observing patterns; AI does a similar thing, but with vast amounts of data.

3. **Understanding Context - Natural Language Processing (NLP):**
   - **Everyday Comparison:** When AI understands human language, it's like having a conversation with a friend who grasps context. NLP enables AI to comprehend meaning beyond words.

4. **Finding Patterns - Neural Networks:**
   - **Everyday Comparison:** Neural networks are AI's way of finding patterns. Imagine connecting the dots to see a picture. Neural networks do this on a massive scale, revealing intricate patterns.

5. **Optimizing Decisions - Optimization Algorithms:**
   - **Everyday Comparison:** Making decisions becomes smoother with optimization algorithms. It's akin to finding the best route for your commute—AI optimizes choices based on specific goals.

6. **Feedback Loop - Reinforcement Learning:**
   - **Everyday Comparison:** Reinforcement learning is like training a pet. AI learns through trial and error, receiving feedback, and adjusting its actions to achieve better results over time.

7. **Handling Uncertainty - Probability:**
   - **Everyday Comparison:** AI deals with uncertainty using probability. Think of predicting rain based on cloudy skies; AI calculates probabilities for various outcomes, making informed decisions.

8. **Processing Data - Big Data:**

- **Everyday Comparison:** Big data is like AI's massive library. It processes enormous amounts of information, finding meaningful insights—similar to sifting through a vast collection of books to gather knowledge.

9. **Real-time Adaptation - Dynamic Learning:**
    - **Everyday Comparison:** Dynamic learning is AI staying up-to-date. Just like you adapt to new situations, AI continuously learns and evolves, ensuring it's always in sync with the latest information.

AI might seem like dark magic for some, but at its core AI is essentially just a collection of algorithms.

Some Computer Science concepts

Binary

While we interact with computers through graphical user interfaces (GUI), command-line interfaces (CLI), or other user experiences (UX), all the information is ultimately translated into binary code (0s and 1s) for the computer's processing.

Binary system is like a digital language with only two words, 0 and 1, but these binary bits can convey complex messages and instructions to make our digital world work.

Take a look at the table below which shows decimal and binary systems.

Decimal	Binary
0	0000
1	0001
2	0010
3	0011
4	0100
5	0101
6	0110
7	0111

8	1000
9	1001

Quantum computers, on the other hand, use a different system called quantum bits or qubits. Unlike classical bits, which can be either 0 or 1, qubits can exist in multiple states simultaneously, thanks to the principles of quantum superposition. This unique property enables quantum computers to perform certain types of calculations much faster than classical computers.

Logic in Computer Science

1. Boolean Logic:

- **What it is:** Boolean logic is like a digital language that computers understand. It's all about simple choices: yes or no, true or false, represented by 1s and 0s.
- **Why it matters:** Computers use these choices to make decisions, like whether to perform a task or not.

2. Making Decisions in Programs:

- **What it is:** In computer programs, we use logical operations like AND (both conditions must be true), OR (at least one condition is true), and NOT (opposite of a condition) to guide the program's actions.
- **Why it matters:** This helps programs decide what actions to take based on certain conditions.

3. Predicate Logic:

- **What it is:** Predicate logic is a way of talking about things being true or false. It introduces variables and statements that involve these variables.
- **Why it matters:** It's useful in computer databases, where you might want to find things based on certain conditions.

4. Making Choices in Programming:

- **What it is:** In programming, we use logic to create conditions. For example, "if" something is true, do this; otherwise, do something else.

- **Why it matters:** It's how programs make decisions and respond to different situations.

5. Solving Problems with Logic:

- **What it is:** Logical thinking is crucial in solving problems in programming and technology. It's about breaking down a problem into smaller, manageable steps.
- **Why it matters:** It helps programmers write effective code and come up with innovative solutions.

6. Formal Methods:

- **What it is:** Formal methods involve using clear rules and reasoning to ensure that systems work correctly and reliably.
- **Why it matters:** It's crucial in developing systems where accuracy and reliability are essential, like in airplanes or medical devices.

7. Everyday Technology:

- **What it is:** Logic is also behind everyday tech. For instance, how your smartphone knows when to display certain information or how websites provide personalized content.
- **Why it matters:** Understanding logic helps us use and interact with technology more effectively.

In a nutshell, logic in technology is like a set of rules that computers follow to make decisions, solve problems, and perform tasks. It's the language that enables communication between us and the digital world.

Algorithms

Key Points to Understand:

1. **Step-by-Step Instructions:** Just like a recipe, an algorithm breaks down a problem into clear, simple steps. These steps tell the computer exactly what to do, one after another.
2. **Problem-Solving Recipes:** Algorithms are problem-solving recipes for computers. Whether it's sorting a list of names or finding the quickest route on a map, algorithms provide a structured way for computers to tackle various tasks.
3. **Efficiency Matters:** Think of it as finding the fastest route to work. Algorithms aim to be efficient, helping computers perform tasks quickly and accurately. Developers design algorithms to be smart and resourceful.
4. **Adaptable Instructions:** Algorithms are versatile. They can adapt to different scenarios. Just like a recipe that works for various kitchens, algorithms can solve similar problems in different situations.

Everyday Examples:

1. **Sorting Emails:** An algorithm can help organize your emails by date or sender, making it easier for you to find what you need.
2. **Predicting Weather:** Weather forecasting algorithms analyze various data points to predict upcoming weather conditions.

3. **Finding the Best Route:** Navigation apps use algorithms to find the quickest route based on traffic conditions.

Why It Matters:

Algorithms are the unsung heroes behind much of our modern technology. They make our devices smart, efficient, and capable of handling complex tasks. So, the next time you wonder how your computer knows what you're typing or how your phone suggests the fastest route home, thank the algorithms quietly working behind the scenes!

Data structures

Key Points to Understand:

1. **Information Storage:** Think of data structures as the shelves and drawers in our library. They provide a systematic way to store and organize different types of information.
2. **Different Types:** Just as you might have shelves for fiction and non-fiction books, data structures come in various types. Each type is designed for specific tasks, making it easier to manage data.
3. **Arrays - The Bookshelf:** An array is like a bookshelf. It stores items (or books) in a linear order, and you can quickly access each item by knowing its position.
4. **Linked Lists - The Chain:** A linked list is like a chain of connected items. Each element holds a connection to the next one, forming a sequence.
5. **Stacks and Queues - The Waiting Room:** Stacks and queues are structures with specific rules. A stack follows a Last-In-First-Out (LIFO) principle, like stacking plates. A queue follows a First-In-First-Out (FIFO) principle, similar to waiting in a line.

Real-World Analogies:

1. **Library Catalog System:** Imagine a library's catalog system as a data structure. It helps you find books efficiently by categorizing them based on genres, authors, or topics.
2. **Kitchen Drawer Organizer:** Your kitchen drawer is organized to make finding utensils easy. Similarly, data

structures ensure quick access and retrieval of information.

Why Data Structures Matter:

Efficient data structures are the backbone of many applications and technologies. They enable computers to process and retrieve information swiftly, optimizing the performance of software and systems.

Operating systems

Key Points to Grasp:

1. **The Manager of Tasks:** Think of the operating system as the manager in an office. Its primary job is to oversee and organize tasks, ensuring that everything functions seamlessly.
2. **User Interface - Your Desk:** The user interface is like your desk. It's what you see and interact with – icons, buttons, and menus. The operating system provides a comfortable workspace for you to perform tasks.
3. **File Management - Your Filing Cabinet:** Just as you organize files in a filing cabinet, the operating system manages files on your computer. It helps you create, organize, and retrieve documents efficiently.
4. **Memory Management - Your Desk Space:** The OS manages your computer's memory, allocating space for running programs and ensuring they don't interfere with each other. It's like making sure your desk has enough room for different tasks.
5. **Task Scheduler - Your Calendar:** Imagine having a calendar that schedules your daily activities. The OS does this for your computer, coordinating when each task gets its turn to run.

Real-World Analogies:

1. **Traffic Signal at an Intersection:** Picture the operating system as a traffic signal at a busy intersection. It controls the flow of tasks (vehicles) to prevent chaos and ensure a smooth operation.

2. **Concierge in a Hotel:** The OS is like a concierge in a hotel, managing requests from guests (applications) and making sure everyone gets what they need without conflicts.

Why Operating Systems Matter:

An operating system is the backbone of your computer, orchestrating its various components to work harmoniously. Whether you're writing an email, watching a video, or running a complex program, the OS is behind the scenes, making it all happen.

In essence, the operating system is the silent manager that turns your computer into a well-coordinated workplace, making your digital experience user-friendly and efficient.

Updates: Your Digital Armor: Much like a knight dons armor for protection, regularly updating your devices and software serves as your digital armor. Updates often include patches that fix known vulnerabilities, making it more difficult for cybercriminals to exploit weaknesses.

Your Digital Identity: In the digital world, your personal information is your most valuable asset. Be mindful of what you share online, limit the data you expose, and consider privacy settings as your shield against unwarranted intrusion.

The Collaborative Effort: Cybersecurity is a collective responsibility. Governments, organizations, and individuals all play a role in creating a safer digital environment. By staying informed, practicing good digital hygiene, and supporting initiatives that promote online safety, you contribute to the collective defense against cyber threats.

Cybersecurity

The Digital Battlefield: Think of the internet as a vast landscape—a space where your personal and sensitive data traverse daily. This landscape, however, is not without its challenges. Cybercriminals, akin to modern-day pirates, navigate this digital sea with the intent to exploit vulnerabilities and pilfer valuable information.

Common Cyber Threats: Understanding the adversaries helps us comprehend the importance of cybersecurity. Malware, phishing attacks, ransomware, and data breaches are the marauders of the digital realm. They seek to infiltrate your defenses, compromise your data, and, in some cases, demand a ransom for its release.

Your Digital Fort: Now, picture your cybersecurity measures as the walls of a fortress. These defenses include robust passwords, two-factor authentication, and regular software updates—simple yet effective ways to fortify your digital stronghold.

Navigating Safely: As you navigate the digital landscape, consider your internet habits as a ship captain navigating treacherous waters. Be cautious about the links you click, the emails you open, and the apps you download. Vigilance is your first line of defense.

The Role of Antivirus Software: Imagine antivirus software as the vigilant guards patrolling the gates of your digital fortress. These tools work tirelessly to identify and neutralize potential threats, acting as a crucial layer of protection.

Computer science sub subjects

1. **Coding (Programming):** Think of coding as giving instructions to a computer using a special language. It's like teaching your computer to perform specific tasks. You can create websites, apps, games, or even make a robot follow your commands by writing code.
2. **Computer Networks:** Imagine your computer can talk to other computers, just like you chat with friends using a phone. Computer networks are like the roads and highways that allow information to travel from one place to another.
3. **Computer Engineering** is like being a tech expert who designs computer brains and creates cool gadgets. It involves solving digital puzzles and leading innovations such as robots, virtual reality, and the Internet of Things. Think of it as the backstage pass to shaping the future of technology
4. **Cybersecurity:** You know how you lock your diary to keep it private? Cybersecurity is about protecting computers and information from bad guys who might want to do harm. It's like putting a magical shield around your computer.
5. **Artificial Intelligence (AI):** Picture a robot that can learn and make decisions on its own. AI is like teaching computers to be smart and make decisions by themselves. It's the magic that powers self-driving cars and helps you discover new music recommendations.
6. **Databases:** Think of a database as a huge filing cabinet where the computer stores and organizes information. It's like having a magical book that keeps track of everything you need to know.

7. **Software Development:** When you create a new app or a game, you're doing software development. It's like being a wizard who crafts a spell (software) to make the computer do exactly what you want.

8. **User Interface (UI) and User Experience (UX):** Imagine designing a game or an app to be easy and fun to use. UI is like deciding where to put buttons, and UX is about making sure people enjoy using what you create.

9. **Big Data:** Sometimes, there's so much information that it's like trying to drink water from a fire hose! Big Data is about handling and making sense of massive amounts of information, like figuring out trends from all the posts on social media.